# THE MEATGIRL WHATEVER

COVER IMAGE
*Victorian Doorstop*, Amy Sollins.

Cover design by Cara Turett
Book design by Rebecca Wolff

Published in the United States by Fence Books, Science Library, 320
University at Albany, 1400 Washington Avenue, Albany, NY 12222

WWW.FENCEPORTAL.ORG

Fence Books are printed in Canada by The Prolific Group and
distributed by Small Press Distribution and Consortium Book Sales
and Distribution.

Library of Congress Cataloguing in Publication Data
Hatch, Kristin [1980- ]
the meatgirl whatever/Kristin Hatch

Library of Congress Control Number: 2014932361

ISBN 13: 978-1-934200-72-8

FIRST EDITION
10 9 8 7 6 5 4 3 2

Fence Books are published in partnership with the University at
Albany and the New York State Writers Institute, and with help
from the New York State Council on the Arts and the National
Endowment for the Arts and the Fence Trust.

# THE NATIONAL POETRY SERIES

The National Poetry Series was established in 1978 to ensure the publication of five poetry books annually through five participating publishers.

Publication is funded by the Lannan Foundation; Stephen Graham; Joyce & Seward Johnson Foundation; Juliet Lea Hillman Simonds; The Poetry Foundation; and, Olafur Olafsson.

## 2012 COMPETITION WINNERS

*the meatgirl whatever*, by Kristin Hatch of San Francisco, CA
Chosen by K. Silem Mohammad, to be published by Fence Books

*The Narrow Circle*, by Nathan Hoks of Chicago, IL
Chosen by Dean Young, to be published by Penguin Books

*The Cloud that Contained the Lightning*, by Cynthia Lowen of Brooklyn, NY
Chosen by Nikky Finney, to be published by University of Georgia Press

*Visiting Hours at the Color Line*, by Ed Pavlić of Athens, GA
Chosen by Dan Beachy-Quick, to be published by Milkweed Editions

*Failure and I Bury the Body*, by Sasha West of Austin, TX
Chosen by D. Nurkse, to be published by HarperCollins Publishers

# THE MEATGIRL WHATEVER

Kristin Hatch

SELECTED FOR THE NATIONAL POETRY SERIES

by K. Silem Mohammad

FENCE
BOOKS

ALBANY   NEW YORK

# CONTENTS

# ACKNOWLEDGEMENTS

many thanks to these journals for publishing some of these poems:

*Black Warrior Review, Can We Have Our Ball Back?, Colorado Review, Court Green, Cranky, Dispatch Detroit, Fence, Forklift, Ohio, Indiana Review, I Thought I Was New Here, Lo-Ball, The Madison Review, Oh No!, Painted Bride Quarterly, Phoebe, Pool, Quarterly West, Shampoo.*

YET WE ARE SMALL AND AS
TERRIFIED AS WE ARE
TERRIFYING IN OUR
FEROCIOUS
APPETITES.

KATHERINE DUNN
*Geek Love*

ANOTHER WAY TO USE
A LARGE HEART ...
IS TO GRIND IT.

M. F. K. FISHER
*How to Cook a Wolf*

# MEATGIRL TRAINING SHIFT #1

greet your eater within a minute, basket in hand.
say, hi my name is (storm cloud, viking, etc.) & i'll be
  your watcher today,
then place the meat with a side of white sauce always
  at four o'clock to the salt.
most of the job is mastering the squat.
it's against policy to sit, but we have to be eye-level.
you can use the edge of the table to help you down, but you get
marked for holding on past that.
your thighs are violin wire.
once in position, let your arms dangle (don't put them in your lap),
  they like that best.
open your mouth wide.
your eater should see fur down your throat.
you have to stay like this as long as he eats.
sometimes after they try to throw the bones in your mouth.
don't get mad.
they think we like it, like they're telling us we're doing good.
if management sees, they'll tell them to stop,
but never tell them yourself—we aren't supposed to speak in position.
your mouth gets dry & the job is boring.
i pretend my mouth in jewelry box scenes:
penguins dancing, marching band parades.
once, this guy complained to management that my stare
  wasn't believable.
his mouth was volcanic. i gagged twice during the session.
they gave me a warning.
i often dream in chicken skin.
like the sun has it on. like
everyone's faces are fried & i have to bite them off.
but it's good money & the other girls are fine.

# KITCHEN

sometimes i forget that my kitchen isn't The Kitchen. today i found chef in mine, grumps. he said i was fat & i said i just wanted some strawberries, but instead he gave me old cheese that was hard and translucent in parts because i put the plastic wrap on wrong. in The Kitchen, this would never happen. & strawberries riper than god. in The Kitchen you can eat all your hunger out. you can have forever in your teeth & you never need to chew. in here, chef likes to mess with you. he likes to make you name all your meats one-by-one, then say every piece of lettuce. in The Kitchen, you just say sandwich & they give you The Sandwich. in The Kitchen, only the people you hate are fat & chef unties your apron just to get his hands close to your butt. flirt.

# THE BITCHES

when it's not busy i usually stand around making jelly tin forts with host. host is high school & i think a racist but he's better than the bitches. the bitches just scowl & puke out ranch at you. host smells like sweet & rancid, teenager smells. he stares at your boobs & gets boners right there at a booth. but he's still better than the bitches. the bitches try to bite your arms off. they nibble at your armpits, packs of them like dogs but they do it in babytalk. they gnaw into your ticklish parts with pitch & favors. they cover you with their goopy mistakes & they make you wear ugly, steal all your fourtops *get it, he's indian* & you just have to build this fort so sound no can find you & you just have to shrink in & wait. one day, you won't smell like mop & they'll still be bitches with hostbabies & you'll be bigtime, you'll ask for everything special & then leave pennies down their slimy bitchthroats.

# CHEF

he's got mannerist hands with moonmouth nails & when he pastries there is the spine like a wind-up tickle-board. he's a big brick building & sturdy & fierce. his precision bulges like an arch at you, push, push. you beg on his balustrade, finding excuses to ask for extra pink sauce or feathers. his answer always grunts & always ramekin fast. chef is dutiful, though aloof. beg. how his fingers, a mini-dice ballet, all of them tap & grab & twist & slap. think. smooth, girl—& thicken at the blade.

# ACCIDENT

then all the dishes flung out of my arms like ballerina-retards. chef
was cutting the eyes off a pink thing—the head was on the garbage
bin—when the crash happened & happened. *jesus bloody hell* he said,
his jaw a concrete overpass. *fuck* with his knife up like he was think-
ing up the thickness of my throat. *jesus.* i smile-dared. chef is scared
of sounds. chef likes it clean in the kitchen. i like to make my messes
there, my graffiti-wild, my sloppy songs. *bloody hell* he said, he chop-
chop said. chef's a highway, a promise full of lonesome roads.

# SIGN OF THE BEEFCARVER POEM

my wrist collapsed & the full pan fell, covering a fourtop at table fifteen w/beets. the empty tin on the floor teeter-tot-rocked like a radio storm. then quiet. their mall-people faces dripped with slabs of heart. aproned, i stayed trophyhead-still while the dadman yelled with his hands branched, a cougar defense like The Beef was The Wild. loud-loud, blah-blah. sorry, sir. i am very sorry, sir. i understand, sir. they tried to make me cry for their beets like the wet would wash their clothes back. after, mashed potato boss man hugged me like the whole united states. i was wrapped up in his map. rolls on his belly like cowboy smiles. mashed potato boss was a kind man. lemon, fork, coffee, coffee, decaf. lemon, fork, coffee, coffee, leeba, leeba. decaf. liver & onions ran out & then stringbean got fired for smoking weed in the deep freeze. some fat, pimpley dish-kid fake-spanked my ass but he did it dumbslow so i felt his sweaty chub hand there like an organ alive next to my butt & then they hired stringbean back. i ate a piece of coconut cream pie & then some old guy asked what i thought heaven was like. like being covered up in pie, i said, clouds of it. leeba did the hard part of closing with the pans without me even asking & all the bent customers left, coughing something burial. leeba & i counted all the money while stringbean shouted a song about how hard it was to be a black man but stringbean wasn't black. he kept singing. we stuffed envelopes of money in our pockets. leeba & i sat in her escort in a medical supply store parking lot in our Beef clothes drinking beers & smoking cigarettes until we thought we saw a cop car & left.

it was summer out, jelly-thick. even at night,
your eyelids were wet with it, how the movies
made it seem

& young, the fist of so much time—we drove.

# SIGN OF THE BEEFCARVER POEM

we were at the break table swatting flies off the au jus. jerky kept laying his bald

head on my shoulder & i was like *i'm trying to eat my french dip*,
   but probably so timidgirl it sounded like purr, purr.

(everything sticky, everything tan) the boys would smoke
   in the kitchen & probably
ash in your au jus.

i mean, don't we all want to be adored, but sometimes you just want
   a sandwich in some secret
& no heads.

back on the floor & it was sunday afterchurch
so the place was buzz buzz whip/would you like some more coffee,
   sir & no tips
because of the lord's bigger.

& then suddenly smoke. not kitchen boy, i mean war.
i mean scream/boom (real batman right here) poof/tinker/trick,
   trick (still).

when a lady drives into The Beef, it gets real quiet for a while after.

& then you keep eating; you assume no one is dead.

then an old woman climbs, churchclothes/alone, through the hole sorry
& then manager jann (with two n's, mickey mouse tie) says sit down.

& the cartoon-ties all talking in a circle & the lady at the big
round table in the smoking room, telephone/accident.

you say *it'll be okay* like you know anything & like she asked
or like it will. but it probably sounded like purr, purr.

& then you just wait around it

& their faces & the big hole by the fake fireplace looking out
    to the parking lot.

# MAGIX BASKET SUNDAYS

for five dollars you get a plastic basket filled with deepfried magix
or hamburgers in tiny, tasteless medallions & a clear, plastic cup of beer.

the magix make me sad because they are so tiny & cute & i used to
    have some as pets
before they started making them for food.
their tiny roars sounded like old man laughs (that kind of cave)
& they would trot up & down your arm for hours.

how is everything in the world tasting.
*wahwahwah, wahwah*: cologne-boy nods, chew-chomp.

the magix are thumb-sized & kind-of gummy.
you can dip them in ranch.
sop it up fatlike in between the hairs of their little manes.

bootleg-baby-chef-in-training just fries a bunch of them all at once
    & turns up some radio nascar shit.
we all want motown but he won't.

sometimes he hums over the dumbshow or yells out *dolls!* or *freedom!* he
kind-of sings *freedom*, but in a big werewolf voice that means not-free,
but also not-caged, more like "i am." too, he bangs around. pots on pots
not on accident, just for loud king, try. he's a big, fleshy man, baby chef
& i don't hate him.

# HUNGER HAVEN

in the walk-in, everything is honest
& stacked in well-marked tubs. you can think about a bath
of cold noodles or death.

they say, years ago, before i was here,
an old lady was eating soup by the window
& then she just died quiet
& they found her still at closing.
on good days, when it smells like green beans here,
    i think of her like a lullaby
& our work, our good work, is wholesome.

in the walk-in it smells young like all the things you
    haven't done yet.

the guy at table sixteen calls himself a regular, but
    everyone here eye-rolls.
he calls you by name & says it a lot. the consonants
    ping-pong on his teeth & the vowels
are swear words he likes saying.
one time he told tanya to call him uncle eddie, but
    his credit card says sam.

in the walk-in, your arms cross in front of you for fake winter.
you can sometimes sit on an empty, upside-down tofu bucket.
this whole place is an animal
& here in the walk-in, you are crouched safely in its white,
    panicked lung.

uncle e-thing always wants tepid water with a lemon wedge.
once, i forgot about the ice.

i brought him ice & he shouted & waved his hands a bunch. i was scared he
didn't like me & that any second he'd
    ask for tanya.
& my face burnt & suddenly i wanted him to think i was pretty.

in the walk-in, it's like stagedeath in someone's arms,
that booming tenor showtune. because sung-to is more comforting
than being the singer for obvious reasons.

you have to cut a whole lemon if it's lunch and the bar isn't open yet
& if the bar is open they get mad at you for stealing their lemons. i mean,
it's just a lemon. you can handle a lemon & the bar really doesn't care.
it's just uncle blah-blah & how you've already given up
just to say his name & eddie-sam likes that & that one time, how you were.
it makes you blush to think of it, so you just shut up & don't.

in movies, that moment before a buck gets shot & either lives or dies
depending on the storyline.
how its face turns to the gun & hush.
you are crouching in its lung.

# BECAUSE OF HIS WHITES

chef looks cleaner than you
& so you want to say *sorry chef*
with more organ.
it feels very sanitary,
to apologize
about onions or the width of your wrist.
he thinks you're a daisy in your dumb
daisylady pants & mostly
you are, but you need just as much proof.
no one likes to be boundless.
you need a special sandwich
to say today is tuesday
& tomorrow will be wednesday
& i will try very hard to make it
because there will be a different kind of lunch
with different sounds, harder sounding
or swooping with lilts.
you tell chef you're sorry
& then he gives you the finger.
this is church.
you flick a crouton at his face.
we are all daisy ladies
because we die regular,
so really, who cares
about how your hands aren't right
or the pale in the middle of your little bottom lip.
it is thursday & to somebody
& that means the DMV or cancer.
*sorry chef,* then more vamp
like you're taught to *i didn't mean to*
(blink, blink) *i swear* (walk away;
hear him watch you).

# THE BIGGEST THING IS HOW EVERYONE IS SAD

on the bus it's just full of sad, faces for pudding.
there was an old couple across on the vertical seats & i kept making
    eye contact on accident with the man.
his suit pants had smaller width pinstripes than his suit coat. anyhow,
me too. it's because when my days end there is no music like in movies
    or serial tv.
you think i am joking. but i'm not. i mean, i do kid sometimes. but really,
    i am about the music.
it's just how in movies people have these hello-personalities, big dolls except
that you don't have to move them. it makes you feel lazy & like everyday is
just one saggy day.

oh, but i was saying about the bus. it was like here we all were on the bus
    to dying.
& people would pop off like extras on a vampire show & we were all just
becoming grayer. then suddenly a lady comes in on the bus just beaming
like it's her birthday except you can tell it's not because she less smug than
birthday & prettier. days are just her bright, bright carnival.
she knows the bus driver/of course she knows the bus driver.

some problems that make me sadder:
beauty pageants for little girls
in general teenagers & our parents hate us all (eyeroll)
when elephants die
war movies on tv
being sad
when other people are sad from something i am not sad from

oh, but so then she walked in, this lady full of nurse, she was like "i am your
sunniest three-o'clock." & i know i should have admired it & maybe did in
a way. but also, slapslap knowing she was so twinkle, twinkle. which then
made me feel worse, like fleshy & like a bad person & it makes sense why any
family hates itself or buildings falling down.

the lady, the old sad lady with the pinstripe suit man, said that she
thought maybe this might be the last time she saw donny. i wondered if
she thinks because he'll die or she'll die. to be so plain about it is either
wonderful or terrifying. she knew the math.

like the last time i saw david fisher. there were only so many times & i
am still sad about it, but only sometimes. not the everyday heavy way. i
     know david is tv & doesn't exist.
but he is my family.

maybe omegas.
everyone sad-looking should eat more fishes. everyone stuffed with
     silver fishes, cartoon catlike.
maybe we'd be a limitless, limitless major chord church song!

sometimes when i see a bus-full i want to touch them & sometimes i
     want to punch them.
i mean, maybe if we just maybe said hello sad, i am sad too. maybe it'd
     feel less lonely and more

like fields & fields of tulips!

*come with me to the fields & fields of tulips!*

we'll just appear in them suddenly.

& the fields & fields of tulips will exhale for us.

maybe fields & fields tulips are the only thing worth not being sad for.

they are so good & kind to grow for us & droop for us when it's time.

tulips & david are the only things there for us. like really there, lodged.

*come with me to fields & fields!* please, david.

14

# CITY SADTHING

i.

i keep trying to stuff words into you,
like they might fill you up with guts or teddy bear cotton

you'd be soft then

(less broken into)

i remember that certain type of night
like your dark was darker than other dark places

without so many parking lots


ii.

i want to call you baby
like how sometimes people say
*will you get my coat baby*
& somebody does & it feels good to get it
punctuated
says: *his tongue feels mountaintop, i know it a tongue's worth*

one day you asked
when you still had teeth without holes, or least when i didn't
    taste them,
*do you like me or the idea of me*

both i said


(like i was ever that sentimental)

iii.

post-coitally, what
gem would you be—
(you were lying thick with me then,
thoracic in the thunder)


i pillow said emerald
you said onyx

(yawn)

ever a seventh grade tough kid
ever a baby in leather


iv.

*baby*


v.

disaster,

we could get married & tangle our debts

(i dare you a thousand rome postcards)


command poem: *get me my coat, baby*


wish you were here

# CITY OF (THE PRODIGAL)

buildings like old men with bent backs. joy curves. curtsy in scape &
window. you were brilliant. you were courtly. we (o we) through the
carcass, the mathwork of metal—we felt so big then, but small in your
tinkering oceanic, next to your honkhonk & bottleface. you tipped your
hat kind & i giggled graffiti, shy against such sky. pet, your pitter-pat, i
unfolded like a map.

it is safer to feel darkly (about, to break within). knots. or lots w/gravel.
padlocks. knuckles & how sometimes when i bleed for months, the
winter sinks into, uterine. inside my snowglobe is city & ache for the
babies i didn't make. i carry the nothing roundly in my gut. i lay my
palm out and bang it where you—

true, i left you in heat that wets for fields so invited (harvest),
    my closest.
false, i left you or ever left you at all.

your operatic coat floated you like a birdthing. flags around the car lot.
fuck, you could be sprightly & jaw. our play castles, our shambles—
bricked magics and the grammar of our shadows—dull, the missing,
a murmuring like radio in sleep. you seep. sturdy & stared. your
howl-guitar (of course you did), such gutter or guttural. your ribcage
masculine evangeline. this city, too: coo, coo.

# BEFORE ALL THE OTHER STUFF HAPPENED

on temperate mornings, the wednesdayed leisure of empty park
benches next to city fountains. gardens that went on like dark fables,
grew rubies. in those days, ribbons hung from bird mouths & if
we pulled them, little libraries inside with tiny wooden ladders. i
couldn't talk then so i pointed & betty unearthed rocks & under,
whole cities. we'd dig for hours through the sun & nap wherever had
us. evenings there were radios from neighboring window screens.
big band, of course. saxophones like stockings. lord, how i loved the
company of those far-away songs, nights that smelled of girl. betty
french-spoke me to sleep (oui, oui cherie) & us waking again, maybe
rain. well, sure there were mosquitoes & the usual jerks, but we had
plenty of knives, apples enough & betty always betty.

# WHEN I WAS GIANT

i was the very best ballet dancer & i wasn't scared. i lept. i wept or
didn't. my plié, the cliffs. every lift, a throat. my eyes alone their tutu
waists. sometimes dainty limbs or the whole sun does; i grew too fast
& gigantic. it felt lonely & then dancing & then it felt less lonely. my
spine, an apse. of course spectacle (aren't we all, aren't we always) of
course thunder. but mostly ocean, mostly home. & you know what: it
took courage. they say the music is in the legs & lord, i had it mighty.
i wasn't delicate, but i was precise & gritty colossal. we all outgrow
ourselves. my enormous arms still perk triangular at the simplest of
songs (a baby's cry, a car alarm). my lungs, my envy.

# CORPSE FLOWER
*titan arum*


the fat borneo of his spadix spread,
made of me a bedsheet relic:

how magdalene was my firefrill,
how eyelid monstral

as he rose up
a thick, thick thigh

exhibit: i laid flawless as a smile—profuse,
profusely blossomed

but how meat & rotten egg of him
to tie me two days tantric.

# BROKEN TULIP

blushed, i bartered this horticultry
(i wanted so bad to be that sophisticated type)

*give me two, will you—*
*i'll be more expensive*, i said in my lazy
bulb head, *cultivate me with a name.*

she pet the soil as i squinted complete.

& i felt the colors rush,
as she sewed sweetmeat coins to my feet
& sketched the wings of me tucked up.

read: the invention of the both-flower.

in the morning i broke of dirtsugar and lake,
& found her prayers pressed on my bloodface

*store me*, i said
*in a dark and not damp place*
*adore me with your coldish*

*i'll be this one-day discovery of yours, if you*
also at my stem.

# VOODOO LILY
*amorphophallus rivieri*


voodoo lily—she was good to me
& i was cut for her, too.

she laid lady in her lazy lip
& curled down round for the darksome

as i crawled long & mouthy, sank
to tuck right
tip-toe into her smug plum.

the rest was the predictable rapture & after

& in the insect of her eyebranch,
i spanked her sweetly, winked.

# OPERATION

it didn't hurt when i carved the long *y* in your chest. you needed help there & as i stood over you in my lab coat, we chatted on about arizona, how you love the empty, the canyon. *you haven't been good to your canyon,* i said, thinking witty, removing all the junk you stored there: your puppet-tongue nightmares, your wax candy songs, extra molars. you apologized to me sheepishly, as though your body was our bathroom & you left your wet towel in a lump. *gives me a job,* i popped back, distantly playful, removing a shredded tire from your drum. *you collect like the road.* you apologized again & i felt bad, so i asked about your mom. you said she was happy & i said that was nice.

once everything was in the garbage bag gallons, i said *sit up.* you looked, with your skin splayed, like a big fleshy star exploding. *listen,* i said. you looked concerned. *we are going to have to turn you inside out. the process is painful, but the pain is momentary & it dulls. it's just the impact of the lining against the air. your insides need air. we'll flip you back after, but you'll have to stay like this a week.* you looked sad. i was sad, too. about that pretty face. it was a shame to invert it, all mushy & red. plus, faces are never the same after the treatment. you said you understood, and so i crept into your redcloud & began with the process. you winced when i pulled your arms through, then legs, but we carried on chitchatting about your son until the head.

after the flip, you said about love. but you didn't mean it. i mean, that much blood can make you say stuff. we were just babies, so i left while you were sleeping, the pulp of you curled up like a heart.

# THE BEDSTAND BURLESQUE

i dozed off during your earlobe liturgy & woke to angels writhing,
shaking their wings off slow. they wound them like western showgirls
then pitched lavishly. one pair flopped over the nightstand lamp & another
landed hamper straddled, boneless. i crawled invisible
off the mattress, stole a pair & headed for the closet. they felt like sandbags
but i strapped them on tight. i thought of the prayers you taught me,
& how i'd bust out: a birthday cake winged-thing, in latin.
but when i peeked, your eyes were froze with flecks of god—they danced
so slutty. so instead i moved a sneaker & all fours sat, thought of
    sick dog heads,
the little plastic funnels on their necks. when i woke again
i woke barking.

# WOLFMOUTH

under the junkyard sky of this brittle-boned place, hope
was smokier yet.

cold windshield (or julytime) you there like a monk (never a monk, still)
while a thousand babyponies thought you could grow them manes
   like library scrolls.
listen. behind your puffup lips, you twinkled (your wrinkles).
in the truck this & that.
in the truck & old goat.

(another ha-ha lolita & the sexpart of your neck—really, an origami crane)

out of the cab of a red f-150: *ooh baby*
*love, my baby love i need you, oh how i need you*

when you smiled big: rows of black tulips where you should have had teeth.

oh my animal thief (loudly—my, my, what weak), i'm grown.
bring me w/your grayish wiles, your dote & leave

& the dearlittles, the sweetest hums—tuck them into my cloak,
this bright-okay as i make a bouquet

& safer, just   to keep them safe.

# THE GINA DAYS

because inside gina, snowglobes. hundreds & hundreds. you wouldn't believe
how many plastic bridges (shake it), evergreens, princess vacations.
gina would become.
gina would the clouds.
gina would the handsomest palm.
gina forever.

pant, pant sigh then. when gina
stilled. it was a big, big still.
everyday tic-toc, succulent leaves, whatever tea. shhhhh!
today is gina's sleeping day!
think about mud. think about looking in kitchen windows at dusk, what
it must feel like alone in the very middle of an ocean, active verbs.

(the housecoat is a warning, dumbass /// shut up, so what)

sometimes night just happens on things. nights happened on gina
& night & night—until boom again: a conch shell locked in glitter!
    hello sunshine! frank sinatra, hey, superbabe whoopwhoop!

so what. worlds explode & then they don't:
birds with bad wings, winter amaryllis, crap dinner, (o) gina (where
    are you now).

# PHOTOSHOOT

*hello, my godface, my ancient one!* yes
my lips are elegies, thanks.

i am a skyline full of me.

*you are a skyline full of you!*
they pep, they pump.

everywhere, dinosaurs—all of them
limping or sad. *this must be a joke.*
i mutter to the bent pterodactyl at my neck,
he just caws there, a bastard caw.

in the pinchwork & sallow
paste of the flash, i pout.

the translator sucks on my pinky.
a man's voice keeps saying like housepaint:
*yes, maria, more feed him!*
*more angry in your hand!*

& then god invented me & me.

# PRETTY POEM

& how light my arms are to think of this
like rich—i am so rich: look
at all my perfumes and my big spain, spain.
i dressed in this splendid frock for you.
do you like how it slopes & shoots.
i mean, the architecture of my skirt is massive & these shoes,
pointy buildings! are my ringlets still in rings?
but really, is my nose a rose? sometimes
when you see something beautiful, your lungs
become people. cheekbone people.
i could eat salads all week, i swear.
i'm cold.
would you like to discuss great literature?
nevermind, you're stupid.
nevermind, i'm stupid.

fancy, i've loved you forever.

i want to eat that tv lady's shoulders.

# POEM

we had stomachs enough,
& deathink, that white was predatory, pussed

appetite like ocean, that broke (frill) & over
broke (frill) & broke (frill) & broke

we'd peel our knuckles back to stop it,
how the mouths kept, the waves—
gaping & collapse.

but together, we held hands to stave off the fiend
& strength, our stiller
than so much rock.

but some babyteeth keep.

look at your wrist.
remember how tiny in our cuffs

how we trembled (frill, frill) trembled—

# THE BRIDGE

you can have as much wild fennel as you like here & nothing
is stray enough to care for.

pink house! yellow house! the trees look like costumes!
(you are a costume: for instance, look at your pants).

we keep celebration cooking so the windows fog you in & to
    feel taken care of.
whole hams, the constant breads, anything with gravy or deep sauces.
not beets. i mean roux. i mean thick.

we once wore silk dresses next to pools bright as a mascot.
everything was light then.
the future was a movie of slender women with severe hair.
the future was ferris wheels. all your favorites saints.

we said names out loud for mouth & maybe.
we said words like *one day*. we said please pass the cold cucumber soup.

we were less reticent & death-obsessed.

we were happy for each other's happy & collected preferences
like cardshop birthday ceramics. pistachio, the color red, tuesday.

(which is to say, choose & choices)

but then everything got mild.
for instance, the leaves never came.

oh sure, there is butter enough & denim.
but it's freezing & all the children are just children.

was there ever a pool with water like halved fruit?

was it ever so hot it felt like pressing?

was there a time when we ever didn't—at least a little—consider it?

# POEM

lithe, ever so: burst. not rifted
nor raucous. just leg, a cursive or kind-of.
point & animal splay.
collarbone, my crocus, do you remember winter?
for instance, the way sunlight sucks under.
just forget it—the push
tongue in "tulle," the oh in "orion."
smooth facebone or martyr.
as if the cold was healthful, silky even.
when she was softer, the way a promise
was less precise. when feathers grew.
i know right? like we could ever bow.

# LITTLE

remember when we found that spine
lodged behind the sun's trachea & fenced the clouds for dibs

nature liked us like whimsy nieces
auntie always playing dead

we were see-through then
eager for mud
& the misadventures of the angel zoo—

how to grow thighs thick w/tender

we kept knocking on the glass of elephant grief,
anxious for a word that said like 'cathedral'


alone at night in winter, in a sign-language city

i keep taking pictures of arches.

# MARCHPOEM

without warning, it was spring.

women had sun discs for heads.
babies were growing daisies for fingers. heavens,
& the dogs were everywhere, sad & multicolored.

we could run until the windmill.
we could rip up the grass as proof.
we could, all together, just this once—

this type of green can happen,
this whole.

# SOMETIMES MY ARMS BEND BACK

you owl-tied, pet

a whole tinkertown of leaf & left
our hearts, such filthy birds, as whistles.
we were all ready to jump for the prettiest piano
pound, but the trees nodded against us

& over & over we plink-plunked, we
unhinged our bodies like wafted things
for the sound of fork against crust—something
for certain, crushed.

rubbernecked, in the meat of this monster-suit
at the oilhole,
the muck of our laura-lungs
you were the darkest part of our bigger dark.

we were looking—all—for velvet-throats
begging to get our bobs out, just

*bite the bullet, bayyyyybyyyyyyyyyyyyyyyy.*

# PORCH POEM

in the old hands of those nights
we held out for a day when the sky
had less math. or at least.
those darks were guttural & our lion's yawn:
everything teeth, we all were in that jaw
& undereyes like digging.
(something was setting, something buried
but softnesses are softnesses, still)
in the white parts, wet.
not sad-wet, just wet-wet, the always-wet,
the bigness of witness, miss.
i climbed into laugh volcanic & full
of blankets, built house, right into
the peal. our home
is lovely (do you like what we did with that nook)
but more in the voice. come here
you choirs & choirs. bury us back in.

# PAUL GIAMATTI'S FACE

you were my straight-up swoon.
i was your gushing (toile) boho.

you in the breakfast nook playing gloom banjo.
like ever.
me cutting sly.

we added up & over time.
we need no mums. better, azaleas. you said azeleas
or hell or i did. or hell.

too, this one time i made you smile.
the badlands, crampons.

what's native or not, think teeth, paul. think wild.

whatever, c'mon. let's punch it out:

look, there's you in light with your anxious face,
me to the left against the asphalt hobo
clowning.

& you still, sad as old bones, your country
cheek lifting up. whatever

you're weird; we were darling when.

# THERE IS ONLY JOEY POTTER

you are her face like the weather.
you are the exact thrill (just tug) of her hair.

in this scene, everything by the lips.

& all that filthy hope tied up for god,
blinking, the seaside suns up.

listen, you are not the storymaker is the thing;
this is not your surgery.

ugh, the pain face/i don't like pain face.

i know it sucks. shoulders much—
all these damn campfires, brambles.

you're bound, sure: you are
a flower (any type) of her. you are
her very best skin.

you'll eat all the evergreens by the creek,
then the sorry ache.

but in time, you'll alice.

you'll happy all her birthdays; happy total-bye.

but too, your north, that neck
how houses smell like home or they don't.

# FOR MADELINE

in france, the figs are better figs!

the windows on buildings are baby mouths!

in france, france is an eyelid closed & all those lashes!

you cathedral into—
you creature, bent out on ledges in your best lioness!

in france, the lilies have teeth!

the charms, the charms!

the sky is full of knowing!

in france, everyone is sad!
apple-faced schoolboys sing your lovelier suicides into the sun!

the other ones, they do not discuss in france!

rather, they fade into photographs you tack next to your tiny sinks &
creams!

the photographs have such surprising color!

the rain smells like salt!

o you must! o in france!

(you become everything & everything)

churchbells!

# SNOW WHITE

i blame my pearly skin; it covers me like morning.
the pines bend down for it.

you should see how the owls
nod. it's freaky. i am not the owls.

& yes, my voice is corinthian,
my eyebrows are rich, rich domes, but still:
it's upsetting (or knives).

my thighs curve up like a tulip cup, too much.
do yours? my wrists are not mugs.

they think our bodies are mostly wicked.

& mama just—it just happened to her because
i guess it just happens.

fuck this fleshy pageant. i want to pierce
something fierce.

this is my humble castle. we are
the humble castle.

# ARIEL

my tail was more emerald than emerald, softer
& my sisters—

together, we were mightier than motown. we threw
down like red sunsets.

our bathing songs got us through the briskest!
our mouths, the perfect houses.

i mean, we all make choices.
it's just part of the changing.

up here, it smells clear.
there are too many angles, the food.

all in all i take comfort in the flowers. they rise up
like whispers, all tube & bursting.

there is a field past the grounds & a field past that
& then a field: foxgloves forever.

& when he goes heavy with his dumdum
breath, i trample through them with my enormous legs,
the thick of them, the stiff.

my nightly, to pluck the bulbs off & squish them.
they sound like my sisters singing.

my feet don't feel like burning then,
my quieter end stops aching.

# CINDERELLAS

cinderellas are specialer: hair in ringlets, intrinsic. for instance, their
friends the birds! they're quirky in the most precious ways. they bite
their lips! they love cinnamon gum (how gemstone & fresh). they move
to atlanta! they wear bright skirts! yes, cartoons! yes, more sparklers/
more salt, more garlic!

we wayward princes hunt their otherness. they play hard to get. but
then they show us their ankles! the proposal of their incessant ankles!

that they are alone in their varied crises bodes well. their isolation
makes it easier. if best-friends have to (hello, dormouse), hope them
superhot models or third-grade teachers with potty mouths. note:
regular women reinforce cinderella realness.

authenticity! america! denim skirts!

cinderellas have knowledge obsessions: world war one, detroit techno
djs, how to survive disaster situations. cinderellas go la-te-da.

cinderellas are tortured, but manic. their huge smiles are the void. climb
in. they accept the nothingness & guide us though our boring, brooding
years. adventures! they serve for the good of our kings to come. they
make us go spelunking, do yoga, forgive our fathers. truly, cinderellas are
freaks in the streets, sheets. our mothers call them spunky. all that heart!
all that wild!

but not too wild. cinderellas reign us like dinner. their sole satisfaction
is our rightful cheer. but please be gentlemen about it. this means
gratitude. this means the toilet paper roll. but remember that
pumpkin-y midnight? this means leaving & then letting them knock on
our batmans.

in that way, we rescue them back. & in this way, our debt is paid
for the lessons in lights!lights!lights!
because princes, listen up: no matter what they say (rape culture,
labor wage) all girls love getting saved.

# NARRATIVE

once, we were full of everyone of us. you guys
don't even know.

life was cut flowers out loud.

of all things. of all truly
spectacular things (hot pepper, flight, cashmere robes)
we had more songs than all the songs.

for instance, the body all full of fall. the perfect
long of light.

i mean, sure. but you were there,

violins,

we were never singular.

# LOVENOTE TO MY UNDERTAKER

that you would have known the dead.

i pushed callalilies down my throat
so the flowers would surprise you,
& marked the carotid with your calligraphy tattoo,

sealing my small organs in your suggested jars.
but of course, i know we don't die
like that anymore—

you just have to prepare a body.

how to reconstruct wrinkles
after the flesh is infused with that plastic kind of grief
(anger)
makes a good show.

mourn it to me like you mean it, now.
when you leaned in,
did my corpse push back

you lie so pretty
now, how much did you love me in the neck.

# LOVE POEM

if you were a thunderwhip harp sound
i could play just by thinking about bridges
& if you could see swamps through the windows in your feet
or your neck as a doric thing & if you cooked me
dolls & put them in wax paper for lunches
or if you kept little trees pruned like donkeys, monsters
in your lungs just for me, pets
—if you were an angle i made with fluorescent math
or maybe if your hair smelled like oak tree leaves
& your words always weighed a penny in my hand,
your beard was just felt, or
if you could give me a shatterproof body made of pearl inlay,
like if i was a gun
(am i a gun) a beautiful gun
& if your eyes were compasses that said to the sandcastle city
or if you think this poem is too violent
& when we crash or rot slow or if there is a shush
sometime & if we could (your neck is a doric thing)

# FENCE BOOKS

## POETRY

| | |
|---|---|
| *House of Deer* | Sasha Steensen |
| *A Book Beginning What and Ending Away* | Clark Coolidge |
| *88 Sonnets* | Clark Coolidge |
| *Mellow Actions* | Brandon Downing |
| *Percussion Grenade* | Joyelle McSweeney |
| *Coeur de Lion* | Ariana Reines |
| *June* | Daniel Brenner |
| *English Fragments   A Brief History of the Soul* | Martin Corless-Smith |
| *The Sore Throat & Other Poems* | Aaron Kunin |
| *Dead Ahead* | Ben Doller |
| *My New Job* | Catherine Wagner |
| *Stranger* | Laura Sims |
| *The Method* | Sasha Steensen |
| *The Orphan & Its Relations* | Elizabeth Robinson |
| *Site Acquisition* | Brian Young |
| *Rogue Hemlocks* | Carl Martin |
| *19 Names for Our Band* | Jibade-Khalil Huffman |
| *Infamous Landscapes* | Prageeta Sharma |
| *Bad Bad* | Chelsey Minnis |
| *Snip Snip!* | Tina Brown Celona |
| *Yes, Master* | Michael Earl Craig |
| *Swallows* | Martin Corless-Smith |
| *Folding Ruler Star* | Aaron Kunin |
| *The Commandrine & Other Poems* | Joyelle McSweeney |
| *Macular Hole* | Catherine Wagner |
| *Nota* | Martin Corless-Smith |
| *Father of Noise* | Anthony McCann |
| *Can You Relax in My House* | Michael Earl Craig |
| *Miss America* | Catherine Wagner |

## PROSE

| | |
|---|---|
| *Prayer and Parable: Stories* | Paul Maliszewski |
| *Flet: A Novel* | Joyelle McSweeney |
| *The Mandarin* | Aaron Kunin |

## OTTOLINE PRIZE

| | |
|---|---|
| *Inter Arma* | Lauren Shufran |

## MOTHERWELL & ALBERTA PRIZE

| | |
|---|---|
| *Negro League Baseball* | Harmony Holiday |
| *living must bury* | Josie Sigler |
| *Aim Straight at the Fountain and Press Vaporize* | Elizabeth Marie Young |
| *Unspoiled Air* | Kaisa Ullsvík Miller |
| *The Cow* | Ariana Reines |
| *Practice, Restraint* | Laura Sims |
| *A Magic Book* | Sasha Steensen |
| *Sky Girl* | Rosemary Griggs |
| *The Real Moon of Poetry and Other Poems* | Tina Brown Celona |
| *Zirconia* | Chelsey Minnis |

## FENCE MODERN POETS SERIES

| | |
|---|---|
| *In the Laurels, Caught* | Lee Ann Brown |
| *Eyelid Lick* | Donald Dunbar |
| *Nick Demske* | Nick Demske |
| *Duties of an English Foreign Secretary* | Macgregor Card |
| *Star in the Eye* | James Shea |
| *Structure of the Embryonic Rat Brain* | Christopher Janke |
| *The Stupefying Flashbulbs* | Daniel Brenner |
| *Povel* | Geraldine Kim |
| *The Opening Question* | Prageeta Sharma |
| *Apprehend* | Elizabeth Robinson |
| *The Red Bird* | Joyelle McSweeney |

## NATIONAL POETRY SERIES

| | |
|---|---|
| *the meatgirl whatever* | Kristin Hatch |
| *Your Invitation to a Modest Breakfast* | Hannah Gamble |
| *A Map Predetermined and Chance* | Laura Wetherington |
| *The Network* | Jena Osman |
| *The Black Automaton* | Douglas Kearney |
| *Collapsible Poetics Theater* | Rodrigo Toscano |

## ANTHOLOGIES & CRITICAL WORKS

*Not for Mothers Only: Contemporary Poets on Child-Getting & Child-Rearing*
Catherine Wagner & Rebecca Wolff, editors
*A Best of* Fence: *The First Nine Years*, Volumes 1 & 2
Rebecca Wolff and Fence Editors, editors

# LA PRESSE

CONTEMPORARY FRENCH POETRY IN TRANSLATION

EDITED BY COLE SWENSEN